Pr(

CREATING CONTA

also by Andrea Shapiro, Ph.D.

MW00365783

It is very easy to have good intentions, and even easier to get advice from someone who has good intentions. What is hard is to recognize the landmines on the path to successful change. *Creating Contagious Commitment* helps identify and think about such obstacles before we encounter them, making the path to change more thoughtful and ultimately more successful.

—Dan Ariely, Ph.D., James B. Duke Professor of
Behavioral Economics, author *Predictably Irrational*

The Tipping Point is a brilliant computer model of change initiatives as they unfold in large, complex organizations. Change agents need to be informal, keenly aware of the different needs of different types of people, and committed to their purpose. This book shows what to do and what happens along the way, both in the model and in real life.

—Art Kleiner, author, *Who Really Matters* and
The Age of Heretics

Driving and sustaining change in large organizations is difficult and time consuming. Many change initiatives end in failure and frustration. There is no easy remedy for this, but Andrea Shapiro has provided us with a well defined roadmap. We have successfully used both *Creating Contagious Commitment* and her computer simulation in many of our internal training programs and change initiatives.

—Bill Vick, MBL, Global Operations Development
Manager, ABB

—Jaime Trevino, Ph.D., Global Operational Excellence
Program Manager, ABB

It is only by effectively influencing people's beliefs, values and changing social norms that we can change behaviors that get us all to "yes." Andrea understands this and clearly maps out how new cultural norms can be systematically embedded into any organization. This book is a must have in any change agent's toolbox.

—Peter Faill, M.Sc., Corporate Procurement Manager,
Durham County Council, United Kingdom

Innovative methods used for introducing the concepts of organizational change to employees are both fun and creative. What really stands out with this book is its accessibility; its direct applications to the world of work; and its practical strategies for effectively managing organizational change.

—Michelle Shields, Ph.D., Fulcrum Associates,
Christchurch, New Zealand

Andrea Shapiro sets the "change table" and doesn't forget a thing. Linking and integrating change levers, she creates a complete blueprint for rebuilding an organization's culture.

—Kathleen Ponder, Ph.D., Global Director, Duke
Corporate Education

For the first time, it is feasible for the majority of change initiatives to succeed! An articulate and accessible approach.

—Tim Dempsey, President, TimDempseyConsulting

This book is a starting point for anyone involved with leading or driving a business change. Once you have a sense of the levers that are key to spreading change, you will be ready to consider your business change in a far more realistic light.

—Roger J. Bushnell, Business Performance Specialist

Andrea Shapiro, Ph.D.

CONTAGIOUS
COMMITMENT
at WORK

Applying the
Tipping Point to
Organizational Change

Foreword by David Yarrow, Ph.D.
Director, Time for Change

Published by
Strategy Perspective
Hillsborough, North Carolina
www.4-perspective.com
ccc@4-perspective.com

ISBN: 978-0-9741028-3-2

Library of Congress Control Number: 2016903064

BUS103000
BUSINESS & ECONOMICS/Organizational Development

CONTENTS

FOREWORD

In *Contagious Commitment at Work*, Andrea Shapiro recounts stories about organizational change that match our experience. She brings principles and relationships to life through examples and builds a model in our minds that help us better understand and influence the world.

Conceptual models are a strong basis for good nonfiction writing. Some models have depth and rigor, conscientiously building on the established body of knowledge in the relevant field. Others are highly practical and understandable, helping us know very clearly what we need to do and how we need to do it. Some models are cleverly designed to outline areas in which we should focus our thinking. They enhance our analysis and decision making rather than trying to tell us all the answers. They enable us to take sound principles, apply them to our context, and, importantly, own the conclusions and solutions we develop.

It's a rare model that manages to combine all of these benefits. The model described in this book is one of those uncommon and invaluable models.

Shapiro's achievement is that she has thoroughly analyzed the best available explanations of what happens when we try to make changes happen in organizations—explanations provided by the recognized experts in this field, including John

Kotter, Everett Rogers, William Bridges, and Daryl Conner—and blended together the insights that they provide. In this way she has created an intelligent model, the Tipping Point, of how attitudes to a specific change evolve and how our actions as change leaders can affect these crucial attitudes. She uses this model as the engine of a sophisticated simulation that can bring the consequences of our actions to life. Around the simulation she has built a genuinely effective and engaging learning tool—the Change, Dialogue, and Action workshop—that makes the learning accessible and energizing. More important, it makes the learning fun! This is an excellent example of the gamification of training.

One of the strengths of the ideas presented in *Contagious Commitment at Work* is the universality of their relevance, their applicability to things that happen in every workplace, in every organization, and team. An organization can only change when there are alterations to what it does, how it does it, what it achieves; those things only change when the people who work in the organization change their minds, attitudes, interpretations, and behaviors.

Nothing in the Tipping Point model will enable us to change human nature itself. However, it can enable us to better understand human nature in the context of organizational change and better understand the implications for our visions and plans. Armed with these insights, we are better placed to analyze our context and the changes we are planning and make sure we play to the strengths that are available to us, and at least mitigate the worst unwanted side effects that may arise from actions that we decide to take.

I have spent most of my working life wrestling with the trials, tribulations, and challenges—and sometimes the triumphs and delights—of change management. Working as a trainer, educator, and adviser, I have used a range of different approaches to help others grasp and apply change and change management concepts. I have had the privilege of working with Andrea Shapiro for more than a decade. I have put her ideas into practice, to good effect, in many and various situations and have played a part in supporting their deployment via the hundreds of change leaders and consultants who deliver the workshop worldwide. If there is a more effective change-related learning intervention than this workshop, I have yet to find it. For that reason alone, it is an honor to write the foreword to this book.

David Yarrow, Ph.D.
Director, Time for Change (Development) Ltd
Time-for-Change.co.uk

INTRODUCTION

The world is moving at an ever faster pace. Technology is a major impetus. Constantly increasing computing power drives innovations in communications, biotechnology, information technology, transportation, and a vast array of consumer products. Powerful political, economic, ecological, and social factors, such as worldwide trade, global warming, and emerging markets all affect the rate of change. This frenetic pace means opportunities appear quickly, and disappear—or are seized by competitors—just as quickly.

Organizational change initiatives help businesses adapt to the changing world—or even disrupt it and create markets that did not exist before. The simple fact is that organizations do not change unless the people in them change. Regardless of what is driving an initiative, employee actions and decisions determine whether it reaches its desired results.

Employee buy-in and support depend on understanding the change—both the business case behind it and how it will affect them. When introducing innovations that are clear improvements, it is easy to believe that just as soon as you explain the plan, all employees will be on board. A colleague recounted an experience with just such a belief.[1]

> We were planning a major, company-wide quality program in a multinational manufacturing firm. Improving quality required significant changes in how employees did their jobs, especially in their attitudes toward their responsibilities and the outcome of their work.
>
> Meeting with the project sponsor, I outlined just how new the approach would be. To make this work we'd have to change employees' mindsets, and I had a course of action to make it happen. We would leverage the expertise of a small group of employees with experience in the new methodology. The sponsor cut me off in mid-sentence saying, "I'll write them an email to change their attitudes. Now, where is your project plan?"

---

[1] The accounts throughout this book are adapted from my own and others' experiences to illustrate points made in the book. Some are cited first-person accounts, and some are modified at the request of the contributor. A few are adapted from *Creating Contagious Commitment* or my blog. I am grateful to all who shared an experience.

Hopefully, few managers have such a simplistic belief in the power of an email, despite how easy it would make change management. If an all-powerful email or a magic wand really transformed people's attitudes, then the success rate of change programs would be much higher than the less-than-encouraging 15–50% reported by researchers.[2]

Getting people to use new technologies or follow new methods—not as an overlay to their regular work but as an improvement—is no trivial task. Successful change demands planning, attention, and commitment. Success starts with a clear vision of the end state and aligns the tools and rewards to get there. It encourages employees who understand the advantages of the program to share their know-how. The Tipping Point model of change provides a framework to integrate these components. Leaders have used it to create successful change in a wide range of organizations.

The book you are holding, *Contagious Commitment at Work*, explains the Tipping Point model through the experiences of people who have put it into practice. Stories from the field and testimonials illustrate the model components, the ways they interact, and how to apply them. This book is a companion to *Creating Contagious Commitment: Applying the Tipping Point to Organizational Change*, which goes into depth on the theory

[2] There is more explanation of the research behind this statistic in *Creating Contagious Commitment: Applying the Tipping Point to Organizational Change*, 2nd edition.

behind the Tipping Point model. *Creating Contagious Commitment* grew out of an interactive learning workshop, called Change, Dialogue, and Action, that leverages a computer simulation of the model.

Contagious Commitment at Work focuses on understanding the model through stories, but a brief outline of six earlier models, which influenced the Tipping Point, helps put it into context. They were developed by Kurt Lewin, Marvin Weisbord, William Bridges, Everett Rogers, Daryl Conner, and John Kotter. Each model addresses different aspects of organizational change. All of them had an impact on the Tipping Point model.

Lewin introduced the idea that change requires shaking up the old status quo and providing a framework for a new stable state. Weisbord outlined six interacting factors to understand an organization and make changes in it. He also made clear the need to use both the organization's formal and informal structures. Bridges focused on the time needed for people to go through a series of psychological phases before they can accept a new change. Rogers recognized that each person's decision to adopt an innovation follows a course that unfolds over time. He is best known for describing how individual adoption decisions propagate through an organization from innovators and early adopters through to laggards. Conner identifies two key roles: advocates and sponsors. Advocates recognize the value of the change, and sponsors have the authority to sanction it. Kotter stresses the role of leadership and lays down eight steps for those who lead change.

Six Models of Change that the Tipping Point Draws upon

Lewin—Change is a process that requires unfreezing the status quo.

Weisbord—The organization is a system. Understanding how the components interact is key to change.

Bridges—People need time to go through psychological phases before they can accept a new change.

Rogers—Innovations propagate through an organization by individual adopters' decisions, from innovators through to laggards.

Conner—Two key roles in implementing change are advocates and sponsors.

Kotter—Leadership, at all levels, has a key role in change.

The other main influence on the Tipping Point model is systems thinking, which emphasizes the interactions and feedback loops inherent in the world. It is a discipline for describing interrelationships that shape the behavior of natural and business systems. The Tipping Point model has been built into a system dynamics computer model, which captures these important interactions. You can read more on the influences that systems thinking and the six models have on the Tipping Point model in *Creating Contagious Commitment*.

While the theory is of interest to many, this book, *Contagious Commitment at Work*, paints a picture of the model's practical impact through people's experiences. Chapter 1 highlights the central role that employees have in making a change initiative successful and the dangers of becoming focused only on the tools and processes needed for the initiative. Chapter 2 presents the two parts of the Tipping Point model: the four attitudinal stages people go through as their support of a change evolves and the Seven Levers, which are actions that leaders can take to influence people's attitudes. Chapter 3 relates short, real-world examples of business initiatives. Each story illustrates a different aspect of the model and its impact. Chapter 4 presents four longer accounts from organizations in different sectors. For-profit, nonprofit, large, small, local, and multinational organizations are all represented. Each applied the concepts in the Tipping Point model to their own initiative. These stories, from diverse environments, show how the various parts of the model work together to make changes more successful. Chapter 5 summarizes the Tipping Point model, and introduces the Change, Dialogue, and Action workshop.

Chapter 1

The achievements of an organization are the results of
the combined effort of each individual.
—Vince Lombardi

MAKING AN IMPROVEMENT

At its heart, an organizational change is an idea about getting work done better. Whether about increasing efficiency, enhancing quality, or lowering costs, ideas are spread by people. Learning about a change from a colleague's experience adds unique credibility. The singular value of peer experience puts connecting and motivating employees at the heart of effective organizational change management.

ORGANIZATIONS DON'T CHANGE— PEOPLE IN THEM DO

If employees understand the need for a change and see consistent management sponsorship for it, they begin to work in ways it prescribes. Once they experience positive results, they can embrace change and advocate for it. With the needed tools, rewards, and leadership, employee advocates can spread their interest to their colleagues—allowing the initiative to take root and grow. Any effort to improve depends on employees with a sense of ownership and involvement spreading their positive attitude to others.

There are many ways to improve how an organization thinks about and does its work. Examples of organizational change efforts include adjusting compensation plans to reflect corporate needs, expanding electronic medical records systems, implementing computer-based e-Learning, becoming more customer-focused, merging with another organization, or increasing productivity. These examples are diverse, but they have one thing in common: Unless leaders engage employees sufficiently for them to advocate for it, a change won't spread—regardless of its importance to the business. If it doesn't spread, it's dead.

GETTING FROM HERE TO THERE

When implementing a change, it is tempting to concentrate on easily quantifiable elements such as tools, technology, rollout plans for hardware or software, formal processes, training schedules, and so on. It is common to use these easily measurable aspects as the primary indicators of success. This is confusing the *means*, usually tools and technology, with the *ends*, people using the tools and technology to work in new ways.

Overemphasizing the quantifiable can yield a false sense of progress. Measuring and analyzing can give the impression of progress no matter what is measured. It is easier to count whether a widget is installed than whether it is being used as designed—or even used at all.

The quantifiable aspects of the program cannot be ignored, but they are only part of the picture. The people side of change forms the other half of implementing any initiative. It is about communicating the vision, getting employees interested and on board, preparing them for new roles, leveraging their experience, and rewarding their successes.

Concentrating on the easily measurable—while ignoring people's attitudes and engagement—is a trap. Employees who do not understand the value of the new methods and technology or who have seen too many similar tools come and go without support for using them, are unlikely to pay attention when the latest set is announced. This may account for the dismal statistic that 50–85% of organizational changes *fail*.

Keeping attention on both the quantifiable side and the people side can turn this dismal statistic around. It demands leadership, collaboration, and communication. Most important, never lose sight of your end goal—having both the tools and processes in place *and* employees using them to improve how work gets done.

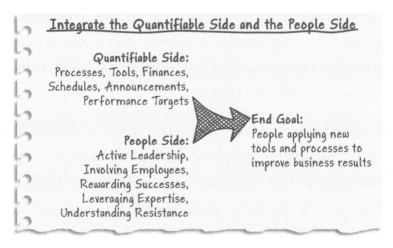

Integrate the Quantifiable Side and the People Side

Quantifiable Side:
Processes, Tools, Finances,
Schedules, Announcements,
Performance Targets

End Goal:
People applying new
tools and processes to
improve business results

People Side:
Active Leadership,
Involving Employees,
Rewarding Successes,
Leveraging Expertise,
Understanding Resistance

Confusing the means with the end goal is not new, nor is it limited to organizational change. Albert Einstein wrote, "Perfection of means, and confusion of goals, seems—in my opinion—to characterize our age." Perfecting the means can require a great deal of energy. Focusing exclusively on the quantifiable side, for example, developing the best processes and then creating schedules and performance targets around them, wastes time and money unless employees are motivated to take advantage of them.

PEOPLE ARE SENSIBLE

When an organizational change program is first announced, ideally you want everyone to come on board as an enthusiastic supporter of it. Employee reaction is often quite different. Employees are not just treading water waiting for the new program. They have a full workload and deadlines to meet. Getting their attention is not easy when the odds of a change succeeding are less than 50/50. Jumping on board a newly announced program does not make much sense when, in all likelihood, a trinket decorated with its logo will be its most lasting legacy.

Given the current success rate, the simple fact is the rational position for an employee to take is "wait and see." If the implementation does take hold, there will be time enough to get on board. You can call this position neutral, uninterested, indifferent, disengaged, or apathetic, but you can't say it doesn't make sense. Any logical person would want to be sure the latest change isn't just another "program du jour" before putting much effort into it. To successfully deploy a change, you want to turn this around. You want the logical position for employees to be getting on board and supporting a change.

A BALANCING ACT

Completing a change demands a balance of both *leadership* and *followership*. Active, committed followers don't appear without visible, dedicated leaders. A compelling, long-term vision is a key part of leadership. It grounds the change program within the organization and gives employees a good sense of what to expect after it is implemented. It helps people understand how the change affects their work and their role in the organization. Vision is a necessary but not sufficient step to getting employees fully engaged as effective followers.

Trusting that leaders will fully sponsor the program and see it through to completion is essential for employee engagement. An implementation strategy, with a concrete rollout plan, sets the foundation for the trust. Aligning the organization with the implementation strategy—by making sure that planning, budgeting, measuring results, and evaluating employee performance are all consistent with the vision—increases trust that leaders are fully behind the change. Regular, two-way communication of successes and challenges keeps the trust going. This includes making sure employees are safe to raise concerns. Unswerving leadership, together with the tools and processes to get the job done, and rewarding employees for doing it, fosters followership. Without steady followers, success is unlikely.

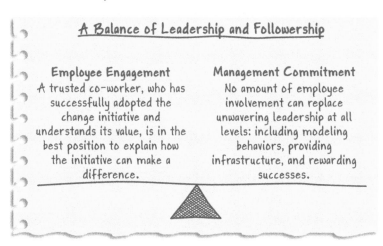

A Balance of Leadership and Followership

Employee Engagement
A trusted co-worker, who has successfully adopted the change initiative and understands its value, is in the best position to explain how the initiative can make a difference.

Management Commitment
No amount of employee involvement can replace unwavering leadership at all levels: including modeling behaviors, providing infrastructure, and rewarding successes.

This is where the Tipping Point model comes in, with its Four Attitudes and Seven Levers of Change. The model provides the framework to help leaders understand how to move employees from an indifferent, wait-and-see position toward one of recognizing its value and even advocating for it with colleagues.

Chapter 2

Reason leads to conclusion. Emotion leads to action.
—William Magee

THE TIPPING POINT: A MODEL OF CHANGE

The Tipping Point model is a dynamic, structured approach for leading an organizational change. It is dynamic because the model recognizes that change does not follow a linear course, in which employees move smoothly to increasing stages of commitment. People may recognize the need for the change, increase their involvement, and begin to adopt it. However, unless they have what they need to succeed, they are likely to become discouraged and lose interest. The Tipping Point model provides a framework that leaders can use to make the choices needed to engage employees and move a change forward.

COMPONENTS OF THE TIPPING POINT MODEL

Many factors influence employees' decision to get behind a change project. The consistency of management support, its adoption by peers, and its perceived value all combine to influence adoption. To capture this, the model has two major interacting parts:

- Employees' attitudes, at any given time, about the value the change can bring to the organization and to themselves.

- Actions that leaders take to endorse the change and back it by providing needed tools and monitoring progress.

First, consider an employee's attitude or viewpoint toward a change. He may feel disengaged or apathetic. She may be its strongest advocate. A third may be in the middle: questioning the change's value or management's resolve to fully deploy it. Another might be actively pushing back, resisting the project or its implementation. These mindsets or beliefs will vary for different employees and can and will shift over time.

You want employees to engage in and advocate for the project. However, they typically start out with a more tepid, neutral opinion of it. This is where the second major ingredient of the model, the Seven Levers of Change, comes in. Leaders use these levers to sway employees' mindsets. The Tipping Point model organizes the Seven Levers and provides a guide to applying them in ways fitting the change project and the company's culture. Successful change leaders use the levers to encourage a positive attitude of commitment to a project— moving employees from disengagement to enthusiasm.

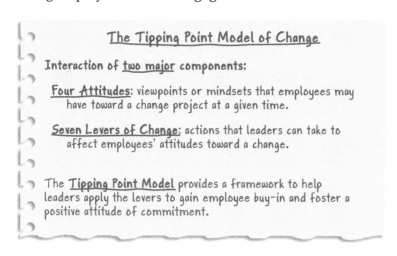

The Tipping Point Model of Change

Interaction of __two major__ components:

__Four Attitudes__: viewpoints or mindsets that employees may have toward a change project at a given time.

__Seven Levers of Change__: actions that leaders can take to affect employees' attitudes toward a change.

The __Tipping Point Model__ provides a framework to help leaders apply the levers to gain employee buy-in and foster a positive attitude of commitment.

ATTITUDES TOWARD A CHANGE

Employees fall into one of Four Attitudes or attitudinal stages depending on their assessment of a change:

- Advocates understand its value, see their role in it, and contribute to its success.

- Incubators are thinking about it and comparing it against how work gets done in their organization.

- Apathetics are unacquainted with it or feel disconnected from it.

- Resisters are actively pushing back against the change.

Through experience with it, **Advocates** have developed a commitment to the change and want to see it take root. Given the opportunity, Advocates explain their experience with the new way of working to colleagues who are disengaged, that is, **Apathetics**. If Apathetics begin to mentally test their experience with current workflow and support for prior changes against the new ideas, they become **Incubators**.

Some Apathetics who hear about the change never incubate it. They might feel overwhelmed by its requirements or underwhelmed by its potential. Without leaders who fully champion the change — that is, explain its value and sponsor its implementation — many Apathetics will either ignore it or nod in agreement but take no action, and thus remain Apathetic.

Employees move from Incubators to Advocates when they gain experience with the change initiative and have support from management. Their advocacy can further spread the initiative. When enough people become enthusiastic Advocates for the new idea, there is momentum to create a positive epidemic of change.

Ideally, Incubators will become Advocates. However, in practice some Incubators will lose interest and become Apathetic again. Still others will become **Resisters** and actively work to undermine the initiative.

No attitude state is a guaranteed end point. Continued support from leadership helps Advocates retain their contagious enthusiasm. Otherwise they may become disillusioned and return to apathy. Conversely, leaders who share their vision of full implementation, ensure that employees have the right tools, and reward successes help Resisters move out of their rut and reconsider the change.

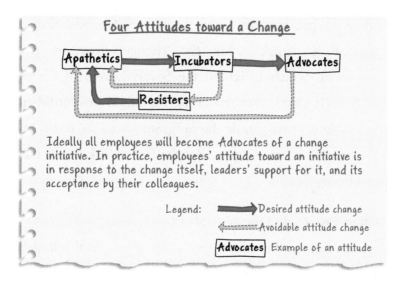

Four Attitudes toward a Change

Apathetics → Incubators → Advocates

Resisters

Ideally all employees will become Advocates of a change initiative. In practice, employees' attitude toward an initiative is in response to the change itself, leaders' support for it, and its acceptance by their colleagues.

Legend: ➤ Desired attitude change
           ⟵----- Avoidable attitude change
           Advocates Example of an attitude

WHAT MAKES THE TIPPING POINT MODEL UNIQUE

Many models recognize that employees go through stages of commitment as they learn more about a change and its potential. In the Tipping Point model, this path (Apathetics to Incubators to Advocates) is the part of the model shown at the top of the diagram above.

The Tipping Point model is unique in going beyond this simple progression. It recognizes that people do not move steadily forward through stages of involvement and commitment. At every step along the path to advocacy, people may slip back to apathy or even into resistance, making the model more realistic and useful. The lighter arrows in the diagram (on the previous page) illustrate the potential to lose commitment and slip back.

The key to progressing from Apathetics to Incubators to Advocates is support for the change program from management, which is where the Seven Levers of Change come in. Seeing the levers in action gives employees confidence that management will guide the program across the finish line. The Tipping Point model provides the framework to use these levers effectively.

INFLUENCING YOUR OWN ATTITUDE

Before reading further about the levers, pause to think about what could affect your own attitude toward a change. What management practices would influence your attitude toward any initiative—whether it is to cultivate quality, streamline the supply chain, or better understand customer needs?

Take a minute to look at the list that follows. Pick the items from it that are most likely to encourage you to back an initiative and help others understand it. We'll return to this list shortly to see its connection to the Seven Levers.

What influences your attitude toward a change initiative?

☐ Having the tools and tailored training to make the initiative effective.

☐ Mass emails or a meeting with all affected employees.

☐ Leaders whose actions demonstrate commitment to the change.

☐ Seeing outsiders, with experience in similar changes elsewhere, hired to implement it.

☐ Acknowledgments and bonuses for achieving change milestones.

☐ Seeing peers who raise problems with the initiative reassigned to areas less affected by it.

☐ Hearing about the initiative's value from a trusted colleague.

INTRODUCING THE LEVERS

What follows is a list of the Seven Levers of Change with a basic definition of each one. The purpose of the list is to introduce the levers. The sections that follow have more details and examples of using them.

- Infrastructure—investing in the tools, processes, and other resources that employees need to be successful with the change initiative.

- Walk the Talk—active leadership is about ownership; it includes making the business case clear, modeling behaviors, clearing obstacles, and making course corrections.

- **Reward & Recognition**—acknowledgment and compensation for employees who work to move the initiative forward.

- **Mass Exposure**—getting out information about the change through broadcast messages or other one-size-fits-all methods.

- **Personal Contacts**—creating opportunities for Advocates to share their experience of the change with peers who feel disengaged.

- **Hire Advocates**—hiring from the outside to gain expertise for the change initiative.

- **Shift Resisters**—moving people to areas less affected by the initiative.

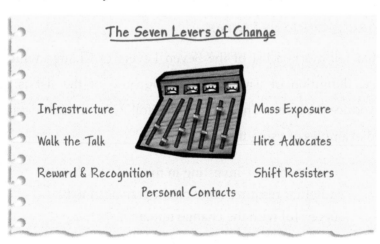

The Seven Levers of Change

Infrastructure   Mass Exposure

Walk the Talk   Hire Advocates

Reward & Recognition   Shift Resisters

Personal Contacts

A word of caution: Don't assume all levers are equal, or that every change initiative benefits by applying every lever. The levers have different effects—and effectiveness—depending on the initiative, the organizational culture, and the phase in the implementation. Perhaps most important, the levers are interdependent. The efficacy of each one depends on the other levers being used.

KEEPING THE LEVERS OF CHANGE IN BALANCE

Using the levers is a bit like using a soundboard at a musical event. An audio engineer uses the same *levers* for different concert halls, different musical groups, or even different audiences. However, he or she would never use the same lever *settings*. The music, band, and venue together determine the settings to use.

The Tipping Point levers are analogous to the soundboard. Effective leaders use settings that fit the organization's shared norms and values, the specific change program, and employees' past experience with change. No lever is a panacea, and none is a pariah. Used together, the levers support both the program and the people expected to change.

Over- or underusing a lever has side effects. Some levers even have inherent negative side effects from using them at all—even when needed. Any adverse effects vary depending on the lever, the program, and the organizational culture.

WHERE IS THE LEVERAGE?

Before going on, please take a couple of minutes to look back on your responses to the questions in "Influencing Your Own Attitude" beginning on page 20. Each choice in the list is an example of one of the Seven Levers. Compare your responses to the following list.

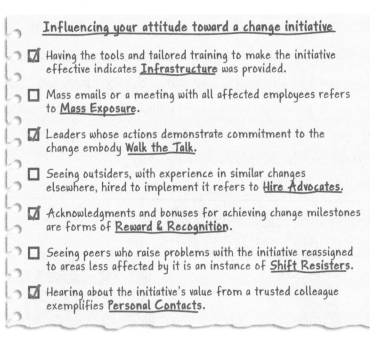

Influencing your attitude toward a change initiative

☑ Having the tools and tailored training to make the initiative effective indicates **Infrastructure** was provided.

☐ Mass emails or a meeting with all affected employees refers to **Mass Exposure.**

☑ Leaders whose actions demonstrate commitment to the change embody **Walk the Talk.**

☐ Seeing outsiders, with experience in similar changes elsewhere, hired to implement it refers to **Hire Advocates.**

☑ Acknowledgments and bonuses for achieving change milestones are forms of **Reward & Recognition.**

☐ Seeing peers who raise problems with the initiative reassigned to areas less affected by it is an instance of **Shift Resisters.**

☑ Hearing about the initiative's value from a trusted colleague exemplifies **Personal Contacts.**

Every other item has a checkmark in front of it, representing Infrastructure, Walk the Talk, Reward & Recognition, and

Personal Contacts. Like most people, you probably indicated that these are the levers you would find most influential. This leaves out three levers: Mass Exposure, Hire Advocates, and Shift Resisters. These are not as influential, but sometimes can be necessary. Delving into examples of the levers in action, the next few sections will make their uses and differences clear.

USING THE SEVEN LEVERS OF CHANGE

Let's start with the four most influential levers. The three Environmental-Support levers set the scene for the change initiative: **Infrastructure, Walk the Talk,** and **Reward & Recognition**. The fourth lever, **Personal Contacts** between Advocates and others, takes advantage of the context built by the Environmental-Support levers to catalyze interest in the change. When these four are used together, they can create an environment that fosters success for an initiative.

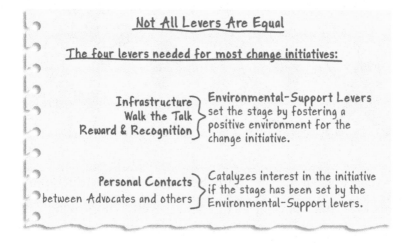

Not All Levers Are Equal

The four levers needed for most change initiatives:

Infrastructure
Walk the Talk
Reward & Recognition

Environmental-Support Levers set the stage by fostering a positive environment for the change initiative.

Personal Contacts
between Advocates and others

Catalyzes interest in the initiative if the stage has been set by the Environmental-Support levers.

INFRASTRUCTURE NEEDS DEPEND ON THE CHANGE

The Infrastructure lever is about putting the tools that employees need into their hands. The specific tools or processes depend on the change program itself. A few examples show the variety of Infrastructure that different programs require.

The Infrastructure to better understand customer needs and develop products to fill those needs includes market research instruments like surveys, focus groups, or prototyping tools. Supply chain management needs methods to define new procedures, software to carry them out, and role-specific training about modifications to workflow.

It is easy to think of more examples. Enhancing quality, reducing the development time cycle, improving the organization design, streamlining hiring practices, or building an e-Learning system all require different Infrastructure.

Role-specific training, designed to help people understand how to perform their jobs under the new regime, is a form of Infrastructure. In contrast, general training that gives high-level information about the program, its value, or the proposed rollout plan is a form of Mass Exposure. A simple distinction is that one-size-fits-all training is Mass Exposure, whereas tailored training to help individuals use the new tools effectively in their own jobs is part of Infrastructure.

Infrastructure is often expensive. At the same time, cutting corners by not providing the necessary tools is counterproductive. It typically undermines the program and costs more in the end. Leaders of a committed business culture ensure employees have the tools they need for the change to succeed.

WALK THE TALK IS ACTIVE LEADERSHIP

Unlike Infrastructure, Walk the Talk is similar for all change initiatives. Its focus is twofold: setting an example and aligning the organization with the change.

Leading by example sets a strong and clear message. Actions and decisions that are consistent with the initiative reinforce its importance. Suppose the goal is to improve quality. Managers who pay attention to volume and schedule but ignore quality in their periodic reviews undermine the change. On the other hand, managers who demand that products live up to quality standards, even at a risk to the delivery schedule, reinforce the importance of the change.

Aligning the organization—the people and the practices—is a big part of Walk the Talk. Ensuring that employees understand the case for change and involving them early in planning strengthen commitment. Aligning Reward & Recognition and Infrastructure with the new direction further encourages employee engagement. Anyone with a leadership role, at any level, has to be on board. Misalignment is perilous to any change effort.

Change brings uncertainty, which increases employees' concerns. Listening to these concerns and addressing them as appropriate are parts of Walk the Talk. Active leadership includes ensuring that employees understand the case for the change—the advantages the initiative offers and the dangers to the enterprise of not implementing it.

REWARD & RECOGNITION HELPS SET THE CONTEXT

Reward & Recognition, which reinforces the right efforts as well as the right results, is the third lever used to create an environment that supports the change initiative.

Reward & Recognition includes both monetary incentives, such as raises, bonuses, and cash awards, as well as individual acknowledgments and other recognition. Acknowledgments can be informal: a public "attaboy," a voucher for a nice meal, or a handwritten thank-you note; or they can be formal: an award ceremony or a promotion. A promotion doesn't just recognize a person's contributions to the initiative; it confirms the change is important to the organization.

The key to Reward & Recognition is aligning it with the initiative. Rewarding people for performance consistent with the status quo, while expecting them to adopt an initiative, is more common than we would like to admit.

Too many of us can tell stories of misaligned rewards. Perhaps it was expecting employees to improve quality, while rewarding them for volume or turn-around time. Maybe it was preaching the importance of teamwork while basing all employee compensation on individual performance. If the change is important, then it's critical to align Reward & Recognition with it.

ADVOCATES ARE YOUR CATALYSTS

When given the opportunity to share their knowledge and experience, Advocates' enthusiasm for a change initiative can become contagious. Fostering Personal Contacts means building opportunities for Advocates to share their experience with the change with people who feel disconnected from it.

Personal Contacts naturally offer space for two-way communication. Apathetics ask questions or express concerns and get responses from colleagues with experience. Discussing the specifics with co-workers is the best way to learn how the change initiative works "on the ground." Peers who know the value of an initiative from experience are the best people to explain its advantages. Fostering contacts between Advocates and their colleagues catalyzes interest in the initiative and helps embed it in the organization's culture.

YOU MIGHT NEED THESE, BUT USE WITH CAUTION

Mass Exposure, Hire Advocates, and Shift Resisters don't have the power of the other levers, but neglecting them is sometimes dangerous. The section titled "Introducing the Levers," on page 21, defined these levers. The following paragraphs explain when they might be helpful, and why you need to be careful using them.

Mass Exposure refers to broadcast messages in any medium. These could be emails, large informational meetings, mass voicemails, glitzy web pages, one-size-fits-all awareness training, or trinkets (such as T-shirts, mugs, key chains, and pens). Some Mass Exposure is usually necessary. It's effective for relaying facts, but it can never substitute for the two-way communication that is part of Personal Contacts. Despite its drawbacks, it might be the most overworked lever.

Next consider **Hire Advocates**. If the change program is new for your organization, you might not have enough in-house expertise to create a strong pool of effective Advocates. Hiring people with experience and know-how in the program from the outside might seem like a solution. However, bringing people in from the outside—specifically for the change—can be demoralizing for existing employees. They suddenly see opportunities vanish for them, or they doubt if these outsiders can be effective because they do not understand the organization's culture.

Consider other options first. Alternatives might include developing internal talent, tying regular hiring (for replacement, succession, or growth) to experience with the change program, or using temporary assignments from within the business.

Resistance to change is real. It might be necessary to **Shift Resisters** to an area less affected by the program. However, shifting or reassigning employees who are vocally opposing the change might create its own problems. Resisters might have valuable information about issues with the implementation that you cannot see from your perspective. Seeing a trusted colleague reassigned, when fellow employees are uncertain if the change will stick, can lower morale. Probably most important, don't confuse apathy with resistance. Resistance may be stealthy or out in the open, but unlike apathy, resistance is active. Resistance is not indifferent or passive. (See "Resistance—In Your Face or Behind Your Back," starting on page 58.)

Pay attention to these three levers, but remember that Infrastructure, Walk the Talk, Reward & Recognition, as well as leveraging Personal Contacts with Advocates, have more lasting positive effects.

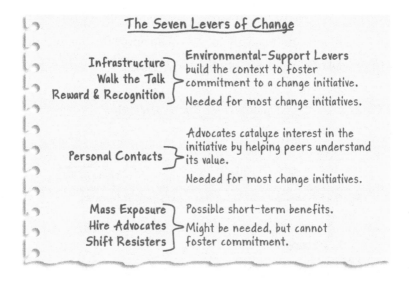

The Seven Levers of Change

Infrastructure
Walk the Talk
Reward & Recognition
} Environmental-Support Levers build the context to foster commitment to a change initiative.
Needed for most change initiatives.

Personal Contacts } Advocates catalyze interest in the initiative by helping peers understand its value.
Needed for most change initiatives.

Mass Exposure
Hire Advocates
Shift Resisters
} Possible short-term benefits.
Might be needed, but cannot foster commitment.

PUTTING IT TOGETHER

To recap, the Tipping Point model has eleven basic components: Four Attitudes toward a change initiative and Seven Levers of Change. To review the definitions of the components of the model, see "Attitudes Toward a Change" (on page 17) and "Introducing the Levers" (page 21).

The diagram on the following page shows how the eleven components fit together to form the Tipping Point model. Recall that the attitudinal stages (or perspectives) people can move through are Apathetics, Incubators, Resisters, and Advocates. Ideally, people's commitment to a change would increase steadily. They would move smoothly from Apathetics to Incubators to Advocates and remain Advocates (shown by wide dark arrows in the diagram). However, as we have seen, people may lose interest due to lack of support for the initiative and fall back (shown by wide light arrows).

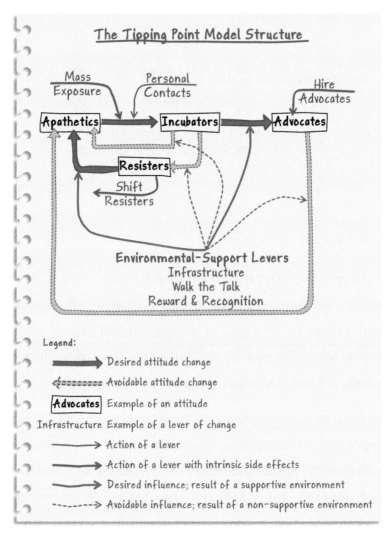

The Tipping Point Model Structure

Legend:

➡ Desired attitude change

⇐======= Avoidable attitude change

| Advocates | Example of an attitude

Infrastructure   Example of a lever of change

——➤ Action of a lever

——➤ Action of a lever with intrinsic side effects

——➤ Desired influence; result of a supportive environment

------➤ Avoidable influence; result of a non-supportive environment

The Seven Levers are actions that leaders can take to positively affect people's attitude and encourage commitment to the change. They are Personal Contacts, Mass Exposure, Hire Advocates, Shift Resisters, Infrastructure, Walk the Talk, and Reward & Recognition. (The lever names are in blue.)

Think of the Tipping Point model as having two steps. The first step, moving from Apathetics to Incubators, is mainly learning about the change initiative and beginning to understand its value. This can come through Mass Exposure or Personal Contacts.

Knowing about the initiative is just the beginning. Employees can never become real Advocates without actual experience with it. Leaders set the stage for Advocates getting experience by using the three Environmental-Support levers: Infrastructure, Walk the Talk, and Reward & Recognition. Infrastructure means that employees have the tools and processes needed to make it work. Walk the Talk gives employees confidence that their leaders fully support the initiative. Reward & Recognition further reinforces that the business is serious about it.

If the Environmental-Support levers are used in ways fitting the organizational culture, then an employee can take the second step and become an Advocate of the change. If the Environmental-Support levers are not used suitably or consistently, people will go back to being Apathetics or even become active Resisters. Even Advocates can lose interest and revert to apathy if they don't see a supportive environment for the change. The Tipping Point model stands out by recognizing that deploying a change initiative is not a simple, linear, forward progression. (See "What Makes the Tipping Point Model Unique" on page 19). This emphasizes the need to consistently use the levers to encourage advocacy and prevent regression to apathy.[3]

---

[3] The Environmental-Support levers, which set the stage for a change initiative, together have an indirect effect on every change in attitude in the model. (See the previous diagram.) In contrast, the other four levers have a direct influence and each lever only affects a single change in attitude. Specifically, Personal Contacts and Mass Exposure only affect the flow from Apathetics to Incubators; Hire Advocates only affects the flow into Advocates and Shift Resisters the flow out of Resisters. To explain more background theory, *Creating Contagious Commitment* 2nd edition (updated 2016) refers to the four levers that only affect one attitude change as Single-Effect levers.

Chapter 3

The boss inspires fear; the leader inspires enthusiasm.
—Harry Gordon Selfridge

MASTERING THE LEVERS

Seeing the levers in action in a real change program is a good way to understand how they work. This chapter gives short, illustrative accounts of using the levers. The first three examples, about Infrastructure, Walk the Talk, and Reward & Recognition, give a better idea of how they underpin (or, if used carelessly, undermine) the environment for a program. Next are examples of the reinforcing power of using these levers together and with Personal Contacts. The last section describes choices involved when using Mass Exposure, Hire Advocates, and Shift Resisters.

WALK THE TALK ISN'T EASY, AND IT CAN'T BE DELEGATED

Walk the Talk comes down to a sincere commitment to the change that employees can easily observe. Warren Bennis said, "Leaders are people who believe so passionately that they can seduce other people into sharing their dream." Attempting to delegate Walk the Talk or even sending mixed messages about the program is a clear sign that leadership is not serious about it.

The following three stories are based on real-world cases. The first case shows positive, productive Walk the Talk. The second case, in contrast, left room for improvement. The last account is about applying good management practices to organizational change.

SENDING A CLEAR SIGNAL

An industrial engineer from a large factory tells the first story. He recounts an example of positive leadership by their plant manager.

> We were in the middle of a major safety effort. It followed an accident in the plant. Everyone knew how lucky we were that nobody had been killed. We got the message, though. After a thorough safety inventory, we started a comprehensive health and safety program.

Line employees already understood the importance of safety—even before the accident. As soon as they figured out management was serious, we began making great strides integrating safety into every action. Employee suggestions became a large part of the input to improve procedures.

One day it nearly fell apart. The whole facility was abuzz when Joe, our plant manager, was cited for showing up on the factory floor without a hard hat.

First violators were required to attend a remedial safety lecture. Joe could have easily exempted himself from it, and nearly everyone thought he would. After all, he wasn't actually running a machine.

There was nearly as much buzz when Joe showed up for the course. Everyone heard that he was an active participant, stressing that safety is everybody's responsibility. His participation at the lecture reinforced that, as a company, we were serious about safety, and no one's "day job" is more important.

You can see from this example the power of the plant manager's Walk the Talk. Joe attending the training had no material effect on the program. The content of the class was unlikely to affect his day-to-day job. However, his attendance sent an unambiguous signal that he and the company were serious about changing and committed to safety. It had much more influence than any email or presentation on safety.

OUT OF TOUCH

Unfortunately, contrasting examples are easy to come by. The following account is a composite, part of which appeared in *Creating Contagious Commitment*. It reflects similar change programs in two companies. Both make products sold to consumers by retailers. The firms had similar experiences trying to update their product lines. The following story, from the viewpoint of a market researcher, outlines what happened.

We had been a leader in personal care products for years. It seemed like market share had eroded suddenly. Management launched a project called "In Touch." The kickoff made a solid case: Our traditional customer base was aging out. Younger customers had different needs, but we were still making the same products. Our senior manager made it plain that if we didn't put more effort into understanding the new customers' needs, then we'd continue to see market share erode. It was up to us.

It was liberating. I led a market research team, and we knew how to run focus groups to explore new product ideas and really understand what customers want.

The salespeople jumped in. They had anecdotes and experiences from retailers that they were ready to run with—without any market research or concrete evidence to confirm their assumptions. It was impossible to make them understand that they had good ideas, but their ideas just needed to be tested and validated.

Then someone hired a human factors team. I'm not sure what sector they came from, but it was not ours. Their ideas about prototyping, products, and packaging were far too complex to be workable in our environment.

"In Touch" ended after a year of too many good ideas and not enough direction or follow-through from our leaders.

The senior manager did a good job of explaining the threat to the future of staying with the status quo. However, he was not close enough to the action to recognize that several teams felt they were in the best position to understand the customers' needs. The resulting turf battles put a strain on the project it did not recover from.

EVERY LEADER HAS A ROLE IN CHANGE MANAGEMENT

A visionary leader can set the stage for a change initiative, but it takes every line manager Walking the Talk to sustain the initiative. Despite this, line managers often back away from their role in an organizational change. The manager might feel like the initiative is outside his or her area of expertise. Experience and capability in their fields brought managers to their positions. They may not have the same sense of competency in change management.

Darlene Flynn is a policy analyst for the City of Seattle Race and Social Justice Initiative, designed to end race-based disparities in city government. She helps managers from departments across the city, whether in planning or utilities or recreation, recognize that their areas have a role in the initiative. Managers can contribute to a future where city policies help ensure that citizens have the opportunity to live up to their potential.

As Darlene describes here, managers become leaders in this system-wide transformation by applying the skills they use every day in their area of expertise.

Broad social change doesn't result from merely addressing individual grievances or delivering programs that provide support services to underrepresented communities of color. It requires adjustment to the whole system that contributes to inequity in access to society's resources.

I help managers realize that the same management skills that they bring to their areas of expertise also apply to creating social justice.

Once the analysis of the system has been completed, and it is clear what areas need changing, their job is good management: making the case for change clear, modeling new behaviors, assuring that everyone knows what is needed and what their role is, and monitoring the results.

It is important to reward positive results. In city government, bonuses are typically off the table, but award ceremonies, acknowledging implementation of new approaches, and thank-you notes are not. Managers who take advantage of these types of rewards are signaling their commitment.

It is tempting to believe that any broad initiative, such as race and social justice, can only be led by the mayor. The mayor is clearly important, but every successful change has many leaders and contributors.

When carrying out a change, managers cannot step away and expect it to simply fall into place. The insight and foresight for the future state may come from a visionary leader. However, the more a change affects people, the more important it is for them to see their direct managers consistently Walk the Talk and follow through to its successful completion.

In summary, Walk the Talk is not only about knowing what needs to change and setting the direction. It means being in front and leading the way. Good leadership balances making the case for the change initiative clear, modeling the new behaviors, and leveraging employee know-how. The clarity and commitment of Walk the Talk signals the importance of the initiative. Otherwise, employees are hard-pressed to believe it is more than just another passing fad.

A SELF-REINFORCING ENVIRONMENT

The Environmental-Support levers reinforce one another. Each is more effective when applied with the others. In simple terms, every dollar invested in the Infrastructure gives leaders who Walk the Talk more influence. Similarly, seeing their leaders Walk the Talk gives more meaning to employee Reward & Recognition. It goes full circle: Acknowledging and rewarding successes increases employees' interest in using the necessary Infrastructure.

The self-reinforcement works in both directions. Having the necessary Infrastructure reinforces Reward & Recognition, which makes Walk the Talk more effective. Walk the Talk

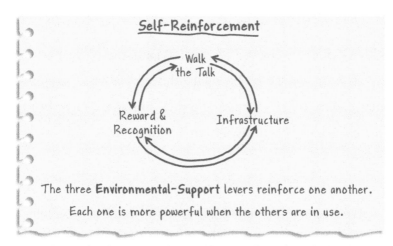

Self-Reinforcement

Walk the Talk

Reward & Recognition

Infrastructure

The three **Environmental-Support** levers reinforce one another. Each one is more powerful when the others are in use.

inherently endorses using the Infrastructure. Collectively they magnify one another, increasing the value of each one.

No single lever can be a magic wand. Used together these levers help create an environment—a culture—that can support any change and move the business toward its goals.

The following three sections illustrate the reinforcing quality of the three Environmental-Support levers. The first two examples provide a contrast. In the first, the leader aligns all three levers to get a valuable employee on board with the change initiative. In the second, an organization tries to use a single lever to implement a small initiative. The last example describes using the levers to create a supportive environment to catalyze the expertise of Advocates.

ALIGN REWARD & RECOGNITION WITH THE CHANGE

Sheldon Galloway owns a residential landscaping business. In the following narrative, he relates how he aligned employee bonuses with the efficiencies of a new software tool to bring a reluctant landscape designer on board with a new bidding process.

We employ talented designers and good crews who produce great installations and pleased clients. Designers are responsible for designing, pricing, bidding, and project managing landscape jobs. Despite good designs, I had to face the fact that our bidding system had too many inconsistencies across jobs. We were overbidding and losing some jobs, and underbidding others and losing profit. This inconsistent bidding made it hard to forecast our future business and profit.

After some investigation I chose bidding software that was created by a landscaper. It was just what we needed. The vendor offered excellent training. It explained how to use the software and the value it brought to the business and the designer. The added efficiencies made the bidding process easier and made profits more predictable. With predictability, I can share the efficiencies through year-end bonuses, which meant designers also saw more consistent and larger compensation packages.

One designer just could not "get with the program." He had decades of experience, a string of satisfied clients, and plenty of excellent designs in his portfolio. I used the software itself to show him its value. I reanalyzed some of his prior bids, so he could see the strength and weakness of each one. He saw his own inefficiencies right away, as well as their negative effects on his personal bottom line. Soon after, he actually sought out the help of other designers to show him how they used the software to be more effective.

In Sheldon's example, the software bidding tool was the necessary Infrastructure, and everyone had access to it. As a leader, he recognized the need to align the company's and the designers' goals to get the most from the tool. When one designer just could not see the value, Sheldon used the software itself to explain its worth to him. He used all three Environmental-Support levers—Infrastructure, Walk the Talk, and Reward & Recognition—to bring a recalcitrant but talented designer on board.

DIRECTION? WHICH DIRECTION?

The following account of attempting to increase a consulting firm's client base using only Reward & Recognition is from a senior employee.

We were close to finishing a major contract when my boss learned of the new policy. The way he explained it, the firm wanted to expand its client base. The firm offered a bonus for responding to requests for proposals from new clients, provided the proposals were accepted. I thought, "Why not?" I had a potential new client in mind.

A colleague and I began planning a proposal. Well, we learned "Why not?" quickly. The proposal writing was an overlay to our regular work. We were on our own! There was no support staff to help explore new areas. No company librarians to help find relevant papers. No money to attend a conference. No admin staff to edit our proposal. We tried to work around these limitations, but they were too big to get around.

I admire the few colleagues who carried through with the writing. There might have been one or two who won a contract. But I'm not sure how big those contracts were, or if they really expanded the client base.

The firm's one-lever, "scatter shot" scheme displayed a lack of commitment that was both nonproductive and discouraging.

Using all three Environmental-Support levers together would be a more comprehensive and strategic approach. Leading the proposal writing efforts with a clear vision of the future direction and future clients, which is part of Walk the Talk, would have been a good first step. Articulating the business case—not just growth but the direction they wanted to grow—is a job for leadership. Once the direction is set, targeting employees with proven abilities in those areas and providing them with the necessary Infrastructure, including time to research and write proposals with administrative assistance, all support the change. Despite its expense, Infrastructure—aligned with the business strategy—becomes a powerful investment. Finally, rewarding the successful proposals, which are aligned with long-term goals, gives further incentive.

THERE IS NO SUBSTITUTE FOR EXPERIENCE

Colleagues with experience in the change have a unique and valuable perspective. A good example of leveraging their experience by providing forums for Personal Contacts with Advocates comes from a Design for Lean Six Sigma (DfLSS) implementation at Xerox Corporation. This account is excerpted from a more comprehensive account written by Heidi Grenek and Norman Fowler and published in *Creating Contagious Commitment* (2nd edition).

Early in the program's development, we focused on identifying existing "pockets of excellence" within the development community. These were individuals who were already using some of the DfLSS principles. We trained these people first, creating well-versed, experienced Advocates who were passionate about their approach. They proved to be a great source of Xerox-specific examples of how the methods and tools could be applied — examples that were integrated into the DfLSS training itself. These examples helped dispute a common myth that these tools could not be used in our products and helped make a better connection to their own problem set for people who were struggling to understand or embrace DfLSS.

These initial Advocates and their library of successful applications also enabled meaningful interaction between Advocates and Apathetics. For example, as the library of successes grew, we started "lunch and learn" forums within each division in which Apathetics and Incubators would get their lunch and eat it while an Advocate was sharing a case study of how they applied DfLSS methods and tools to solve a critical problem. The forums started small, but as the word spread, more people began to attend to find out about this new initiative.

A second example of how this library of DfLSS projects was used to encourage Advocate and Apathetic interactions was the creation of a DfLSS track at our annual internal modeling and simulation conference. DfLSS Advocates were asked to present their projects to the Xerox design community at large, which recognized their achievements across organizations.

> A positive unintended consequence of this recognition was that it strengthened the Advocates' passion for the methods and made them even more committed to share their results with others.

In this example, Heidi and Norm identified the early Advocates of their DfLSS program and helped them become more effective. Using homegrown Advocates was a powerful tool to create additional Advocates across the organization.

A lot has happened in the five years since Heidi and Norm wrote their account of DfLSS. Xerox has integrated Six Sigma into the company's culture, and it has helped reduce costs, eliminate defects, and develop an ethos and language around quality. The integration was so thorough that Xerox no longer has a Corporate Lean Six Sigma office because, as Heidi says, DfLSS has become "the way we work."

MAKING CHOICES WITH THE LEVERS

There is much to consider when it comes to using a lever. For each one, thinking about its strengths and weaknesses informs the decision on whether it is needed. Furthermore, many different actions and decisions fall under each lever. The illustrations in this section focus on the levers that are sometimes needed, but must be used with caution: Mass Exposure, Hire Advocates, and Shift Resisters. Because these levers have intrinsic side effects, the accounts show either problems with applying them carelessly or successes in finding alternatives to using them at all.

SPREADING THE WORD

There are two ways to spread the word about a change program. One is **Personal Contacts** between Advocates and Apathetics. The second is **Mass Exposure**, which is a one-size-fits-all approach.

Leaders can foster Personal Contacts by making opportunities for peer-to-peer advocacy, such as "road shows" or "lunch and learn" sessions led by Advocates (as in the example from Xerox in the previous section). Change networks, where Advocates can learn about effective outreach from one another, reinforce effective ways to engage Apathetics and begin a conversation with them.

In contrast, spreading information from savvy managers to uninformed employees, who are supposed to soak it up, characterizes Mass Exposure. Everyone can give examples of dependence on Mass Exposure or even confusing a big announcement with a deployment plan. This is often more theater than true communication. In communication, a clear message develops from the give-and-take of listening and speaking.

A design engineer from a midsized, privately held firm relates some of the problems caused by the one-way nature of Mass Exposure.

> Everyone was herded into an hour-long talk from the company founder and CEO, a man with a strong, flamboyant personality. We saw and felt his intoxication with a new Balanced Scorecard (BSC) approach. It had a cute acronym that I can't even remember now—despite getting a key chain emblazoned with the logo.
>
> He told us, with flurry and frenzy, that our performance reviews would conform to the new BSC approach. Instantly, everyone went from understanding how their work was evaluated to wondering if they'd ever cash another bonus check.
>
> The anxiety was palpable. He ended his presentation saying, "My door is always open." No one there believed his door was open to their concerns.

It takes a precious commodity—time—to listen with authentic openness to people's misgivings and suggestions for improvement. Integrating those ideas into the program takes even more time and effort. Sometimes implementers, rushed to show progress, believe they save time by pushing ahead with a plan—usually a big announcement—while ignoring employee concerns and ideas. Unfortunately, this is unlikely to save time.

Instead, it hides pitfalls that could easily be exposed before developing into serious problems with costly fixes.

There is a balance between seeking and honoring employee input and setting a program in motion. Foster *open* discussion, but don't let it become *open-ended*. The goal of employee input is to improve decision making, not sidestep it.

YOU WANT RESULTS AND YOU GET CONSEQUENCES

The all-too-common reliance on Mass Exposure usually ends with unintended consequences. Consider another example from a large, US-based service company whose practices, especially for ordering materials, had become misaligned with their reporting structure. They were planning a large-scale reorganization to clarify the reporting hierarchy, simplify ordering, and realign the two.

Like many companies, they kicked off the reorg with a big announcement that every staff member was expected to attend. There were pep talks and a video extolling the benefits of streamlined processes coordinated with the reporting structure. The following account is from a first-line manager right after the big announcement.

> I listened to the lofty benefits expected from the reorganization, and wondered how it would be rolled out and how it would affect my department. I know there is a problem; my manager barely understands my team's work. We are the ones who implement — I should say work around — these misaligned processes in order to satisfy our customers.
>
> Things will be different in my area. I'll be giving up many of my current duties to get others to be revealed sometime ... hopefully soon. I wish that senior managers understood that this reorg could go much smoother if they would listen to my experience.
>
> I will do what I can to make it work, because of my pride. But I see the potential for failure on the horizon.

Employees have career aspirations and personal goals — which are often compatible with the change initiative. This manager's words reveal apprehension that her hands-on know-how would be discounted, leaving her suspicious and reticent about the initiative. She understood the need for realignment long before the announced reorg. She could have been its strongest Advocate. Instead, she felt her experience was ignored while being dictated to from "on high."

Mass Exposure is useful to convey information. However, it is ineffectual when addressing concerns, or helping Advocates spread their enthusiasm. Despite its shortcomings, Mass Exposure is often the first lever managers turn to.

GETTING THE RIGHT PEOPLE

Hiring Advocates specifically to implement a change has plenty of drawbacks, as described in "You Might Need These, but Use with Caution" on page 30. It is better to screen for expertise in the change when hiring for other needs (such as succession, replacement, or growth).

Alternatively, bring in Advocates temporarily from other parts of the organization to seed your pool of Advocates. The following example, adapted from a longer account in the 2nd edition of *Creating Contagious Commitment*, uses this approach. It comes from the National Health Service (NHS) in the UK. Their change program is called Knowledge and Skills Framework (KSF). The goal of KSF is to provide consistent support for learning and development of professional staff, especially nurses and other hands-on healthcare providers. The account comes from Karen Dickinson, a member of the KSF implementation team in the Sheffield Health and Social Care NHS Foundation Trust.

> Initially, I followed the principles of the Tipping Point model in an informal way, using the main ideas as a guide and reference. I worked with people who showed the most commitment—who were already Advocates—and encouraged them to tell their success stories to others. Peers can be powerful Advocates: hearing an experience directly from a nurse rather than reading a directive helped gain commitment from other nurses.

After seeing the value of peer-to-peer advocacy, Karen sought ways to bring more Advocates into her department. She continues:

I made two recruitment decisions based on the principles in the Tipping Point model. Recognizing the pitfalls of hiring Advocates from outside did not alleviate the need for more people with knowledge and enthusiasm for KSF. I recruited two people on short-term posts who had worked in other parts of the NHS on KSF.

Karen avoided the negative side effects of hiring Advocates by creating short-term assignments for people who had experience in KSF from other areas of the NHS. They shared their experiences through peer mentoring networks and participation in training—creating Advocates within her staff—and then returned to their own departments.

It has been nearly five years since Karen first wrote about her experience implementing the Knowledge and Skills Framework in *Creating Contagious Commitment*. Since then, KSF has been streamlined and improved. Sheffield Trust and other parts of the UK National Health Service continue to use it.

RESISTANCE—IN YOUR FACE OR BEHIND YOUR BACK

Active resistance to a change initiative can be covert or overt. Covert resistance is dangerous and easy to miss. Complaining about the initiative or its implementation in the cafeteria, raising and reraising diversionary questions during meetings, or even ignoring planning meetings are examples of covert resistance. Employees may resist covertly because they sense it is unsafe to raise issues openly.

Covert resistance is a problem. Raising genuine issues at the water cooler but not in a planning meeting means they won't be addressed. It is a lost opportunity. The earlier that decision makers learn of a problem, the easier it is to understand and fix it, and the less its negative impact.

The Environmental-Support levers reduce covert resistance by building an environment that makes it easier to voice potential problems. This could be as simple as recognizing employees whose suggestions simplified the implementation, or evaluating all suggestions and taking the time to explain why some cannot be used.

Overt resistance, such as specifically and openly challenging a decision, declaring the change a mistake or a waste of time, or stating an unwillingness to comply, may feel more threatening. Even so, it is an engagement with the change that you might be able to turn in a productive direction. Employees may recognize negative consequences that leaders did not anticipate through assessment and planning, or haven't identified during implementation.

Overt resistance can be an early warning—if it is heard. Encourage overt resisters to define the problems they perceive, and then look into the issues raised for potential pitfalls. If the problems are real, decide how to address them; if not, explain the misperception.

SHIFT RESISTERS OR LEVERAGE THEIR KNOWLEDGE?

The following account is from a senior manager in an engineering company. They were putting a risk management system into action. It involved sharing previously confidential information with customers. He leveraged the knowledge of one overt resister and avoided using the Shift Resisters lever.

> We needed this Risk Management System (RMS). If we were late or had to pull features at the last minute, our customers were at risk themselves. Despite this, I knew there was plenty of discontent. I thought it was because engineers and supervisors had to reveal more information than they were comfortable with—not only with peers and managers but with key customers.

Jack, a very strident engineer who worked for one of my managers, took the grumbling from the proverbial water cooler right into my office. Sharing information was not the problem.

He made a clear case that without having all the analysis tools to evaluate the data we collected, the RMS would fail.

With some trepidation and after consulting with his manager, I decided to give him a budget to evaluate various commercially available analysis packages. He reported on them and eventually procured one.

Once we had the tools that we needed, Jack became the RMS's biggest Advocate. He explained to his colleagues, in terms they understood, how the RMS system worked, what the tools did, and what to expect. His work was pivotal in gaining buy-in from our engineers, a major part of deploying the RMS.

Although sometimes it might be necessary to Remove Resisters from the area affected by the change, Jack's story shows that hearing them out can be more strategic. Acting on his or her concerns may turn a "complainer" into a major asset. A skeptic may have a better plan or a wrong-headed idea, but you can only find out by listening.

Resistance Can Mask Important Information

		Fears and misconceptions	Ideas for improvement
Leadership Response	**Listening**	Misunderstandings and concerns can be addressed.	Potential to uncover superior alternatives.
	Ignoring	Fears are magnified without clear info. Grousing undermines the initiative.	Employees feel disempowered & become less supportive. Missed opportunities.

Source of Resistance

Constructive criticism may contain valuable information. Ignoring fears and misunderstandings only amplifies them. Without listening and understanding the source of resistance, you cannot know how to respond.

If the initiative is inconsistent with the Resister's values or too much of a leap for them, moving the Resister elsewhere can be the most constructive approach.

Chapter 4

To know and not to do is really not to know.
—Stephen R. Covey

STORIES FROM THE FIELD: THE TIPPING POINT MODEL AT WORK

You've read short accounts of applying one or two of the levers in the previous chapters. This is a good way to understand individual levers, but their power comes from using them together in a real-world setting. Each change and every organization is different. Examples provide the best way to see the diverse ways of using the levers together.

The testimonials that follow come from four different sectors. The accounts are from large and small organizations and represent for-profit and nonprofit organizations.

Depending on the business and culture, there are many unique ways to apply the levers. In these examples, look for two things:

- The mix of levers needed is different for the four examples.

- Each lever can involve different decisions and actions depending on the situation.

The first narrative comes from a large, global pharmaceutical company, headquartered in Europe, with facilities in over 100 countries. Their business includes research and development, manufacturing, clinical trials, regulatory reporting, import and export, as well as sales and marketing.

The second account comes from a small nonprofit in Durham, North Carolina. This four-person office coordinates 250 dedicated volunteers to deliver meals chiefly to seniors with limited mobility.

The third account is from healthcare delivery. It is from a Trust in the National Health Service (NHS) in the United Kingdom. NHS Trusts are public sector corporations that fulfill healthcare delivery needs, usually within a specific geographical area.

The last example is from a public charter school in the United States. With a staff of 50 faculty and administrators, this school provides an academically challenging environment for almost 400 middle school students.

A PRESCRIPTION FOR IMPROVING PERFORMANCE

In this account, a global pharmaceutical company sought the best alignment of its people, performance, and products to expand their leadership in the healthcare marketplace. With around 100,000 employees worldwide, this was a significant challenge.

They began by looking at their strengths. In the company, there were pockets of excellence in Lean Six Sigma (LSS) to deliver business improvements. Elsewhere there was strength in project management (PM) to improve execution of projects or in organizational development (OD) to foster employee engagement. To execute their ambitious strategy, they experimented with a fusion of LSS, PM, and OD to create a program they called Accelerating Delivery and Performance (ADP).

Their goals from ADP were to form a structured, disciplined way of working to deliver excellence to their customers. They began by testing ADP in 10 transformation projects, moved to applying it to the whole company via individual business units, and are now working to embed it in all six continents where they operate. Richard Hay is a lead ADP consultant and key agent in the transformation group. He describes using the Tipping Point model to make this happen.

We already had positive experience using the Tipping Point model in a global supply chain implementation. The language of the Seven Levers resonated with our culture, and we expected that it would be useful in ADP. To test this, we delivered the workshop to our core of 20 ADP consultants plus 2 executives. They recognized the value of the framework and went to work creating the "Tipping Plan," using the levers as a systematic approach to measure our areas of influence during the testing phase of ADP.

We reviewed the Tipping Plan monthly, finding that progress on the levers was an effective measure of our progress implementing ADP. Infrastructure, Walk the Talk, and Reward & Recognition are important support for the change, and became a key part of the Tipping Plan.

Beginning with Infrastructure, we created a website for ADP tools. These included the LSS and PM tools as well as the OD elements—based around our defined fundamentals of delivery. The core ADP team itself was a form of Infrastructure. Besides being available to mentor local teams, we also made sure that, as ADP spread, the tools were adapted to different local teams' needs.

For Walk the Talk, we expected the senior ADP steering team to act as role models in the implementation and targeted other senior leaders to become ADP role models. We used the concept of *Gemba* (現場 —"go see to understand") to help leaders be visible to enable the change. We created connections between leaders who were real Advocates of ADP and others who were indifferent or even skeptical. We find that leaders seeing other leaders do something that works is more effective in increasing advocacy than telling them.

Each month, we checked on their performance and helped them make adjustments through coaching. Reward & Recognition focused around ADP excellence awards for outstanding work for teams and individuals. We didn't link bonuses directly to ADP. Instead, we made sure that managers understood that departments that implemented ADP showed better employee engagement on standard company surveys and better business results. This meant that they were likely to see better bonuses through the normal business processes.

Identifying, developing, and leveraging our Advocates, the ADP practitioners, across the business was a major effort. By the end of 2014, we had created over 1,600 Advocates and we created communities of practice for them to stay in touch. They energized one another—working through problems and sharing helpful ideas.

We played down Mass Exposure. There was a monthly newsletter within the ADP community. It was designed less to spread the word about the project to others, and more to keep people already on board informed.

There was some resistance. There probably always is, for any change project. We dealt with it on an individual basis. For each case, we tried to get a good sense of where the resistance was coming from before acting on it.

A challenge we continue to face is the fact that our ADP ways of working were largely developed and applied in the Western world. To have a real effect, we had to find ways to spread our successes to emerging markets in Latin America, Asia, and Africa.

Our unique approach to the Hire Advocates lever in Asia helped bridge this gap, and it is a model we will continue to follow. We created needed Advocates through a combination of one new hire and one temporary transfer. We hired a local person with experience in some of the components of ADP and brought him to the UK to learn about our application by working with the core team. He went back with a second person, who was part of the core ADP team in the UK. This way, no one was entirely new. One person was part of the local culture and familiar with ADP, and the other person was new to the local culture but well versed in ADP.

We are putting all of the Seven Levers of Change into play, as we need them, to spread adoption of ADP throughout the six continents where we do business.

Using the Tipping Point model, the ADP team built on their prior successes with LSS, PM, and OD to further strengthen their market leadership.

Through their Tipping Plan, they used their progress applying the Seven Levers of Change as a leading indicator of their progress with ADP and thus with the business results they expected from it. They used all seven levers. They were careful using Mass Exposure, Hire Advocates, and Shift Resisters—the three levers with the greatest potential for unintended side effects.

The Tipping Point model helped this pharmaceutical company put a well-planned change program into practice worldwide.

FEEDING MORE HOMEBOUND SENIORS

The next successful example of these levers in action comes from the nonprofit sector. Meals on Wheels (MOW) is a US-wide effort to address hunger, especially among older people. They deliver prepared meals to people who are homebound because of illness, disability, or age. With "a nutritious meal, a safety check, and a smile," MOW allows seniors to remain in their homes and communities.

Three years ago, a MOW office in Durham, a moderate-sized city in North Carolina, fed 280 people with a 5-person staff coordinating dedicated volunteers. However, with nearly 100 people on the waiting list, the need was greater than their capacity. To satisfy their mandate, they had to reach more homebound hungry.

The story of how they leveraged the Tipping Point model to expand their reach is related here by Gale Adland, director of the MOW office.

At first, we sought more grant money and to recruit more volunteers. We were fairly successful at this. However, more volunteers means more people to coordinate and a bigger drain on our staff and systems.

After attending a workshop on the Tipping Point model, I began to ponder how to apply the Seven Levers of Change. Infrastructure jumped out as a key missing piece to expanding our capacity. The software we were using was satisfactory for tracking meals, but it was not effective at managing the larger volunteer base or tracking expenses.

I personally began to research software to manage meal programs. With the board's approval, we purchased new software. It not only tracks clients but also helps with volunteer roles, such as scheduling drivers, and has an accounting component to further streamline workflow.

One staff member was trained by the software vendor, and then she trained others. Learning from peers allowed staff to share how it applied to our own MOW office. This personal interaction helped other staff understand the relevance of the tool.

Unfortunately, there was resistance. One employee could not adapt to the new tool, despite efforts to mentor them. A personnel change was needed to move forward. I could restructure and streamline the remaining staff of four people, because the new software increased our productivity.

Six months after installing the new software and using staff to help bring each other up to speed, our small office was feeding 340 homebound seniors. We have increased this level in the intervening three years. We are now able to serve 442 clients.

The Tipping Point was instrumental in deciding to get technology we needed, replace staff who would not adapt to using it, and become a stronger organization.

Compare this example with the previous one. First, note that Gale used a different combination of levers. Infrastructure, Walk the Talk, Personal Contacts, and Shift Resisters made it possible to reach the goal of providing more meals to the homebound hungry. Even when she used the same levers used in the previous example, the specific actions for a particular lever were different in the two different cases.

At first glance, it is surprising that change projects in a worldwide, for-profit company and a small, local charity would have much in common. Both projects rely on new software and processes. Any project that involves new technology can fall into the trap of focusing on the quantifiable side at the expense of the people side of change. (See "Getting from Here to There" on page 9.) In the two accounts, you see how both organizations used the Seven Levers to keep their focus on the needed outcome—improve their workflow to better serve their stakeholders.

LIVING THE VALUES

This example comes from healthcare delivery. The Tees, Esk and Wear Valleys Foundation Trust (TEWV Trust) is part of the National Health Service in the United Kingdom. TEWV has 6,000 employees and serves the mental health and social care needs for a population of more than 1.9 million people in the north of England.

Following a merger and restructure, consultation with stakeholders revealed that the TEWV Trust had become too internally focused, even though working in partnership was one of their core values. Michelle Brown is head of Organization Development for the Trust. She was asked to lead a project called "Embedding the Trust Values." The aim was to create and instill values to support the Trust's goal of "providing high-quality services."

The team's first step was to define the Trust values. They worked with staff, service users, caregivers, Trust governors, and partners to map out five core values. Michelle knew the real danger: the Trust values would just sit on a shelf and fail to inform decision making and actions within the Trust. She leveraged the Tipping Point model to help bring the values to life. As she describes it:

> Research was telling me that if the Trust Board didn't model the values we would not get buy-in from staff. We delivered the first workshops using the Tipping Point model to the Trust Board and senior management. The workshop was very successful in helping them see how important it was to Walk the Talk in their role of leading the change process.
>
> There are leaders at all levels. We developed a three-day Senior Leadership Program, which included the Tipping Point, for staff who reported to directors. It helped them understand the impact of leading by example and of promoting values mostly through face-to-face Personal Contacts, rather than Mass Exposure.

To promote Personal Contacts, these leaders arranged forums for employees to explain how the values affected their own work in the Trust. The small amount of Mass Exposure that we did do used posters with pictures of well-known staff.

We used the Trust values to word all relevant policies, procedures, and employment contracts. This made the values themselves part of the Infrastructure (tools and processes).

Our team set up values-based recruitment— building Trust values into job descriptions for open positions. This further integrated the values into the Trust Infrastructure. It also increased the number of Advocates through regular hiring, avoiding the Hire Advocates lever (specifically hiring for the change itself).

We used Reward & Recognition in two ways. First, the Trust gives annual Making a Difference awards to celebrate staff members' dedication, achievements, and successes. Displaying the Trust's values was used to shortlist potential recipients for the awards. Next, we created an opportunity for peer recognition. Periodic e-bulletins each had a section asking about living the values. For example, "If you know a member of staff or a team who is living the Trust's values, thank or recognize them for making a difference. Please click here to submit your message."

Including the Trust values in performance appraisals led to some difficult conversations. If an individual's performance was not in line with the values, an action plan with quarterly reviews was developed to help them progress. This also reinforced the Walk the Talk lever—helping managers see the power of communicating by role modeling the values.

We contracted with an independent evaluator to gauge employees' awareness and application of the values both in their own jobs, and in their colleagues' and managers' work. Their surveys found consistent growth in both awareness and application of the values as we progressed with Embedding the Trust Values.

Too many of us have been through the exercise of defining values only to have them gather dust on a shelf. Michelle and her team leveraged the workshop to fully understand the Seven Levers. They applied the ones suitable for their change and culture to integrate the TEWV Trust values into employees' daily work.

CONSTRUCTIVE RABBLE ROUSING

Project-based learning (PBL) is an approach to elementary and high school education designed to engage students through working on practical problems. For example, students might learn botany, geology, and horticulture through working in teams to redesign and replant a community garden. Proponents of PBL cite the central role that solving problems and working collaboratively has in students' further education and careers.

Alice, an assistant principal in a public charter school, had the role of helping teachers make the transition to PBL. It takes shaking up to migrate from instructor-led pedagogy, where students have a passive role, to PBL, where students take an active role in their own learning. Alice sees her role as a rabble-rouser. Her job is to encourage faculty to engage in PBL, follow the results, and encourage more faculty to use what works. Her account explains how she used the Seven Levers to help teachers embrace PBL.

Each faculty member was trained in designing and delivering PBL courses to challenge students and help them work together to solve real-world problems. The training produced some gung-ho Advocates, but other teachers were stuck in their traditional—creative, but traditional—methods.

My job is to take advantage of the enthusiasm of the faculty who understand the value of PBL. It means so much more to hear something from a colleague than from me. My "soft power" can be useful to be sure Advocates for PBL have a voice. For example, I assigned one gung-ho teacher the task of taking minutes at a meeting. She recorded every PBL success in the minutes.

Raises and bonuses were not an option. I had to be creative. Two teachers, one in English and one in social studies, developed a humanities course using PBL techniques on their own initiative. I asked them to present their new course as a central part of professional development for faculty. This recognition not only helped other faculty members see an excellent example of PBL, it increased their own commitment to it.

I made sure the value of PBL is always in parents' and teachers' minds. Every letter to parents, whether it was about a field trip or a parent-teacher conference, mentioned PBL goals or successes. It was on the agenda of every faculty meeting. Everyone knew the direction the school was headed.

Alice's school received state-wide recognition for its PBL curriculum. Seeing their students engage with learning, and parents pleased with their children's new problem-solving abilities, became a daily measure of their success.

Choosing suitable actions from the Seven Levers helped make the school's success possible. The initial training for faculty gave them the skills to develop PBL courses, making it an example of Infrastructure. The other levers Alice used were Walk the Talk, Reward & Recognition, and fostering Personal Contacts. These are the four levers needed to implement almost every organizational change.

Chapter 5

The secret of success is constancy of purpose.
—Benjamin Disraeli

MAKING IT WORK FOR YOU

W e know that change is inevitable. Whether it is parchment scrolls replacing clay tablets or tablet computers replacing laptops, new technologies and methods are certain to displace the old familiar favorites. Nonetheless, we can all recite acronyms once touted as business panaceas and now found only on Wikipedia. Academic and field research show that organizational changes often fall short of their goals. In many employees' experiences, they typically just fade away from lack of support and interest.

BALANCING CURRENT AND FUTURE NEEDS

You begin a change program to prepare for future needs, but you cannot ignore current business performance while implementing it. The following story, told by a retired fire chief, lays out this tension. It is familiar to anyone, in any organization, who has implemented a program.

> Change in a fire department is completely different from business. The obstacle in putting a department-wide change into operation lies with the officers. [In a fire department hierarchy, firefighters report to officers, who report to the chief.] Firefighters know how to put out fires. They are busy with what they are doing right now. It works, and they see no need for anything new.
>
> I'm charged with community-wide fire safety. It is a longer-term strategic goal. For example, cigarettes are a leading cause of fire fatalities in the United States. To carry out a cigarette safety program, I need firefighters' active participation. To the public, they are the face of the department. But firefighters don't see it as part of their job. So I depend on officers to enforce firefighter participation. Officers are loath to do so. They have personal and working relationships with the firefighters. Jeopardizing them could affect efficiency and even safety during a fire.

Unfortunately, business is not so different. Midlevel managers and line employees rarely have "line of sight" on the organization's long-term goals. Typically their portfolio and rewards focus on short-term accomplishments. In fact, firefighting is often used as a metaphor in business for solving immediate, urgent problems. You cannot eliminate short-term focus. However, in a competitive, fast-moving business world, you cannot rely on it exclusively.

Organizational changes are designed to support the long-term goals that ensure the future of the enterprise. Making sure employees and managers understand how a change supports these goals is not trivial. There is no clean slate. Prior change programs influence how employees think of the current program.

Choose your change programs carefully. Identify and select only the programs that support the strategic goals of the business. Alignment to future goals clarifies the need for the change. It helps managers understand why a program deserves time and investment and gives an incentive for involvement for all employees from the beginning. See every important program through to completion.

Don't let change initiatives fade away. Either complete a change or formally cancel it. Employees react logically. When one program fades away from leadership inaction, employees hesitate before getting on board with the next one. This disengagement further increases the likelihood the next change will fail. The result is that change programs that could strengthen a company's future fall by the wayside.

Unfortunately, it is a vicious cycle: every time a change program fails, it leads to disengagement and apathy for the next one. This apathy, in turn, increases the likelihood the next one will fail.

Nobody can get inside people's heads to overcome apathy directly. The only way to break this cycle is to reduce the failure rate. Belief that a program will "stick" is an incentive to engage with it, support it, and foster its success. This turns a vicious cycle into a virtuous cycle: each success encourages employee engagement, which in turn, leads to more successes with future programs, as pictured in the following diagram.

Every successful implementation further develops the organization's capacity to change and clarifies its future direction. Applying the Tipping Point model helps you create the successes that engage employees.

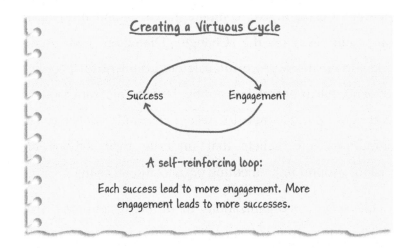

Creating a Virtuous Cycle

Success   Engagement

A self-reinforcing loop:

Each success lead to more engagement. More engagement leads to more successes.

LEARNING THROUGH ACTION

Experiencing the Tipping Point model with teammates in a structured environment is a powerful way to learn its concepts. The Change, Dialogue, and Action workshop makes this possible.

The heart of the workshop is an interactive computer simulation, which is a learning tool that uses system dynamic techniques to capture the feedback loops that make the Tipping Point model unique. Users can set the levers and see the outputs in a simulated organization—bringing the model's ideas to life.

The workshop uses gamification, which brings friendly competition, reflection, and problem solving from games into the learning sphere. It helps people master new concepts by taking advantage of their natural instincts to socialize, cooperate toward a goal, compete in teams, and finish tasks. Using gamification, the Change, Dialogue, and Action workshop creates a powerful, safe environment for people to experience the approach laid out by the Tipping Point model. It encourages participants to recognize and challenge the assumptions and beliefs that underlie their actions and decisions around implementing organizational change.

A wide range of organizations in different countries, from manufacturing to education, nonprofit to for-profit—as illustrated in this book—have taken advantage of the Change, Dialogue, and Action workshop. It helps participants understand the Four Attitudes and apply the Seven Levers to make their organizational change both contagious and sustainable.

WHAT TO EXPECT

The workshop challenges participants, in teams, to devise a strategy that uses the Seven Levers to create Advocates of a change in the simulated organization. Working together on a strategy fosters productive conversations. Participants discuss trade-offs and costs as they settle on a strategy and the lever settings to reflect it. Seeing the results of their work unfold as the Tipping Point simulation runs can be fun. Teams sometimes spontaneously cheer as the computer displays their outcomes. Participants learn from the simulation and one another—making the workshop a low-risk, cost-effective engine of learning and a catalyst for action.

The simulation is not a crystal ball, providing answers for all changes for all organizations for all time. No such magic exists, because no two organizations are the same, and each change poses unique challenges. Nor is the simulation a numeric planning tool. Rather, when used in the workshop, the simulation helps participants experience the Seven Levers and integrate the concepts so they can apply them to their own change initiatives.

Gamification encourages teams to think through interactions and side effects that they may not have considered before. Participants begin to recognize their own and their teammates' assumptions. This helps teams develop a richer, shared idea of the potential range of strategies they might apply, which in turn is key to developing robust deployment plans for their own change.

To get a sense of the workshop and how it brings the model to life, let's hear from two participants. The first account is from a US-based Six Sigma trainer and coach in a medium-sized consulting firm whose focus is information technology.

Making mistakes and learning from them was one of the best parts of the workshop! I listened with my team to the background explanations, and was sure I had it down pat. During the first breakout session, I was surprised that some of my teammates had different ideas about how to set the levers. It took some discussion to hammer out a strategy that we could all agree on. Hearing their points of view added to my understanding.

Our simulated strategy didn't turn out quite like we hoped. Asking questions helped us recognize that we hadn't been thinking of the effects the levers have on each other. The workshop design gave us another shot at creating a strategy and seeing it run on the sim. Our second try turned out more like we expected.

Seeing our own results and comparing them to other teams' results really reinforced the meanings of the levers. I think the workshop made the difference in being able to apply the model with clients.

The second account is from Michelle Brown from the National Health Service in the UK (see "Living the Values" on page 72). She summarizes her personal experience delivering the workshop in support of a major change initiative:

The workshop and supporting materials are cleverly designed to suit the needs of all learning styles. Active learners are attracted to the hands-on "learning by doing," while more reflective learners have access to in-depth explanations and evidence of the underpinning theories and principles. We have seen many examples of "penny dropping" moments as colleagues reflect on their experiences of change and gain insights into what works, what doesn't, and why.

SUMMARY

We know that ideas can be contagious. When ideas are about new and better ways of working, we want to help them become contagious. This only happens when people appreciate the ideas and spread them. The Tipping Point model is the framework to move employees through disengagement and apathy to exploring a change initiative and on to gaining expertise and advocating for it.

All organizations and all changes are unique. The Tipping Point model is generic enough to apply to most change initiatives and specific enough to provide a guide for action, as shown in the real-world accounts in Chapter 4.

The best way to explore and learn the model is through the Change, Dialogue, and Action workshop. It has made a pivotal difference in a wide range of sectors, organizations, and change initiatives. It is an effective and dynamic way to experience the model, and fosters discussion and learning among team members.

To inquire about having a workshop in your organization or learning to deliver the workshop yourself, please visit www.time-for-change.co.uk or strategyperspective.com. You can also send email to info@time-for-change.co.uk or info@strategyperspective.com.

ACKNOWLEDGMENTS

The advice and advocacy of many people made this book possible. My clients and colleagues have taught and encouraged me. Many contributed their experiences to the book, both anonymously and credited; their insights invigorate it.

I owe thanks to Diane Kessler, Jim Killian, April Mills, Carman Nemecek, Leitha Purcell, James Scouller, Pam Weppler, and Dave Yarrow, whose comments on earlier drafts strengthened the message. Special thanks to Annette Shaked, whose judgment and acumen invariably add value, and to Jennie Ratcliffe, who helped me think through so much: from the turn of a phrase to the order of chapters. Integrating input from all of these people improved *Contagious Commitment at Work*. Any oversights are mine alone.

Finally, thanks go to my editors, Laura Poole and Brad Kramer; to Mike Ferrell, who designed the cover; and to Karen Newton for interior design.

ABOUT THE CONTRIBUTORS

I am indebted to all who recounted their experiences for this book. Their narratives enrich our understanding of organizational change and of leveraging the Change, Dialogue, and Action workshop. Thanks to the following contributors and to those whose accounts appear anonymously.

Gale Singer Adland is Executive Director of Meals on Wheels of Durham, NC. She attended Duke University as an A.B. Duke Scholar, with majors in computer science and management science. After working in IT for 30 years, Gale completed a certificate in Non-Profit Management at Duke University and began working in the nonprofit sector. She can be reached by email at gale@mowdurham.org.

Michelle Brown is an organizational change leader with nearly 30 years' experience in the National Health Service in the United Kingdom as a clinician, manager, service improvement specialist and now, head of organizational development. Her passion is applying organizational theory to projects that improve the quality of care. She has used the Tipping Point model in change workshops and leadership development programs since 2010. Michelle can be contacted by email at michellebrown1@nhs.net.

Karen Dickinson is Head of Education, Training, and Development for Sheffield Health and Social Care NHS Trust. She manages the learning and development designing and commissioning training to meet organizational needs, with particular emphasis on the development of support staff. She oversees the use of the NHS Knowledge and Skills Framework; promotes effective performance and development review systems; and supports learning and development in the workplace through in house training, vocational, and academic qualifications. Karen can be reached by email at Karen.dickinson@shsc.nhs.uk.

Darlene Flynn works for the Seattle Office for Civil Rights as a Policy Lead for the City's Race and Social Justice Initiative. In this capacity, she provides strategic planning and training support to the initiative focused on ending institutional racism in city government. She has worked for over 10 years building cross-racial teams that advocate and practice new approaches to bring about institutional change required to further racial equity for communities of color in Seattle.

Norm Fowler was a member of the Xerox corporate Lean Six Sigma Staff with responsibility for developing and deploying Design for Lean Six Sigma throughout the product design community. He is the former president of Keys Six Sigma and the author of *Lessons Learned from an Unconventional Design for Lean Six Sigma Deployment*. He can be reached by email at keywest-norm@outlook.com.

Sheldon Galloway is the owner of a residential landscape design firm in Durham, NC. His gardens are designed to help people connect with nature, connect with each other, and connect with themselves. His emphasis is on native plants, pollinator gardens, and environmentally friendly low-maintenance gardens. He can be reached at sheldon@garden-environments.com.

Heidi Grenek was a member of the Xerox Engineering Center, leading the development of the Design for Lean Six Sigma program electro-mechanical, software, and marketing content. Her focus was on using systems thinking to create a program in which the DfLSS methods, processes, and tools became both pervasive and sustainable across Xerox. She subsequently moved on to other program leadership roles at Xerox. Heidi can be reached at Heidi.Grenek@xerox.com.

Richard Hay has over 25 years experience in the pharmaceutical industry in a career spanning operations, strategy, and business improvement areas. He has been a manufacturing operations site director, leading the site though major change. He currently works as an Accelerating Delivery and Performance lead consultant with a top 10 global pharmaceutical firm. He supports the organization to develop a performance-driven culture through application of Lean, project management, and change management principles and practices. He supports the application of various methodologies including strategy deployment, visual performance management, and applying the Tipping Point to change programs. Richard can be reached via Richard.g.hay@btinternet.com.

David Yarrow has been practicing, teaching, training, and advising in the fields of organizational excellence and change since the 1980s. He leads Time For Change (Development) Ltd (www.time-for-change.co.uk), delivering coaching, support and training in change management, organization development, team building, and best practice benchmarking. He has been leading Change, Dialogue, and Action workshops regularly since 2004, and since 2008 has been a Master Trainer, training and accrediting many consultants and practitioners as workshop facilitators. Contact David by email at david.yarrow@time-for-change.co.uk.

ABOUT THE AUTHOR

Dr. Andrea Shapiro's goal is to help leaders understand the people side of organizational change and optimize their effectiveness through innovative learning methods. She developed an acclaimed interactive computer simulation, called the Tipping Point, to bring effective change management concepts to life. The Tipping Point simulation is an integral part of her Change, Dialogue, and Action workshop, which leverages gamification principles to help leaders understand how to engage employees and gain their commitment to an organizational change. She has taught and accredited change leaders, consultants, and trainers in major corporations, nonprofits, and government agencies worldwide to leverage the workshop. She is also the author of *Creating Contagious Commitment*.

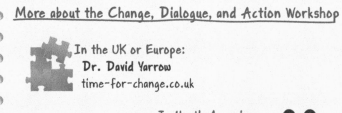

More about the Change, Dialogue, and Action Workshop

In the UK or Europe:
Dr. David Yarrow
time-for-change.co.uk

In North America:
Dr. Andrea Shapiro
strategyperspective.com

Arrange a Change, Dialogue, and Action workshop in your organization, or become licensed to deliver the workshop yourself.

CPSIA information can be obtained
at www.ICGtesting.com
Printed in the USA
LVOW02s2301021016
507077LV00011B/97/P